Building Upon a Rock

Letters of John Quincy Adams to His Son on The Bible and Its Teachings

The ministry of Christian Heritage Fellowship, Inc. is made possible through the generous contributions of friends who seek to promote America's Christian heritage. Your contribution will enable us to continue to reclaim our Christian heritage for succeeding generations. You may contribute at the following webpage:

https://christianheritagefellowship.com/donate

PRESENTED

TO

With the most sincere wish that its reading
will bear the fruit intended by the author
and that your life may be built upon
the Rock of our Lord Jesus Christ

DEDICATION

To our children, Jessica and Stephen,
and Jonathan and Krista

CONTENTS

Image Credits

ACKNOWLEDGEMENT

Appreciation is expressed to Internet Archive for the valuable service they have rendered with regard to this text and millions of other similar works. Without their service, similar timeless classics would remain dormant in various forms contained in literary archives around the world.

INTRODUCTION:

A TRUE CHRISTIAN FOUNDING FATHER

In his eighth letter to his son, on the Bible and its teachings, John Quincy Adams encouraged his son to, "Build your house upon the rock," a biblical allusion to constructing one's life upon the person and principles of Jesus Christ. As a deeply committed evangelical Christian, Mr. Adams took seriously his responsibility to provide for the spiritual nurturing of his children, and the series of which this letter was a part reflected his dedication to this obligation.

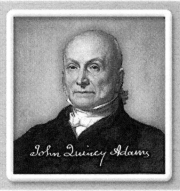

John Quincy Adams

JULY 11, 1767 – FEBRUARY 23, 1848

– GEORGE PETER ALEXANDER HEALY

As a deeply committed Christian, Mr. Adams is remembered as a Founding Father who served his country as an ambassador, treaty negotiator, as both United States Senator and Representative (from Massachusetts), and President of the United States.

John Quincy Adams, son of President John and Abigail Adams, was one of America's most distinguished statesmen who served

2

his country as a treaty negotiator, as both United States Senator and Representative (from Massachusetts), President of the United States, and ambassador to foreign nations.   From his youth, John Quincy accompanied his father on diplomatic missions to France and the Netherlands, and by the age of fourteen was a secretary on a diplomatic mission to Russia. Under the influence of his father, European institutions (such as Leiden University), as well as his alma mater, Harvard, John Quincy became proficient in Latin and Greek languages and the Greco-Roman classics.

When the elder John Adams became America's second president, he appointed his son John Quincy as a Minister to Prussia in 1797, and it was in Berlin, the capital of the Kingdom of Prussia, that George Washington Adams was born on April 12, 1801. Later that same year, John Quincy's family returned to America as Thomas Jefferson assumed the office of president. Over the next decade, John Quincy engaged in Massachusetts politics and assumed a professorship at Harvard in 1805. Then, in 1809, President James Madison appointed him as America's first ambassador to Russia. After successfully negotiating numerous obstacles in route, he finally arrived at St. Petersburg on October 23, 1809.

George Washington Adams
APRIL 12, 1801 – APRIL 30, 1829

– CHARLES BIRD KING

George was the oldest son of John Quincy Adams, the sixth President of the United States. He graduated from Harvard University in the Class of 1821 and studied law, briefly practicing law before being elected to the Massachusetts House of Representatives.

Nearly two years after arriving at St. Petersburg, John Quincy began to write a series of letters to his oldest son, George Washington Adams, who had remained in America to attend school. From 1811 to 1813, John Quincy penned nine letters on the importance of Bible study. Though his primary intent is to provide his son with basic knowledge helpful in the study and use of the Bible, he is mindful of his duty to all his children, and for this reason, asked his son to collect his letters on the subject, saying, "I wish that hereafter they may be useful to your brothers and sisters, as well as to you."[1] Readers studying carefully the content of these letters cannot help but be taken back by the realization that the first letter was written to a ten-year-old, who was likely no more than twelve when the last letter was written.

The Letters of John Quincy Adams to His Son on The Bible and Its Teachings was originally published in 1850, two years after the author's death, and almost forty years after they were initially written. As an apparent indication of the warmth with which the letters were publically received, they were reprinted two years later. The text of this reprint is taken from the first printing[2] with modest attempts to update orthography and punctuation for the benefit of the contemporary reader.

At a time when America's Christian origin has been placed under deep suspicion, it is critical that contemporary voices communicate historical truth with the voice of continuity. That is, fidelity to America's Christian heritage means—in part—that the contemporary message of America's heritage should find continuity with the voices of previous generations. So it is, that in reprinting Mr. Adam's *Letters to His Son*, this presentation edition seeks to unite with the voice of the publisher who first printed this work when he summarized both the character of Mr. Adams and the content of his letters:

> Throughout his long life, Mr. Adams was himself a daily and devout reader of the Scriptures, and delighted in comparing and considering them in the various languages with which he was familiar, hoping thereby to acquire a nicer and clearer appreciation of their meaning. The Bible was emphatically his counsel and monitor through life, and the fruits of its guidance are seen in the unsullied character which he bore through the turbid waters of political contention to his final earthly rest. Though long

and fiercely opposed and contemned in life, he left no man behind him who would wish to fix a stain on the name he has inscribed so high on the roll of his country's most gifted and illustrious sons.

The intrinsic value of these letters, their familiar and lucid style, their profound and comprehensive views, their candid and reverent spirit, must win for them a large measure of the public attention and esteem. But, apart from even this, the testimony so unconsciously borne by their pure-minded and profoundly learned author to the truth and excellence of the Christian faith and records, will not be lightly regarded. It is no slight testimonial to the verity and worth of Christianity, that in all ages since its promulgation, the great mass of those who have risen to eminence by their profound wisdom, integrity, and philanthropy, have recognized and reverenced in Jesus of Nazareth, the Son of the living God.[3]

In the spirit with which this work was originally published, this little volume is once again humbly inscribed to the young men and women of America. May the anticipated spiritual benefit of this volume by one of America's greatest Founding Fathers be yours in the fullest measure possible.

Editor, Stephen A. Flick, Ph.D.

LETTER ONE:

STUDY THE BIBLE

By his own spiritual habit of devotional study, Mr. Adams had set a good example for his son, but in this first letter, he takes the opportunity to formally encourage him to study God's Word. Above all other forms of reading, Mr. Adams encourages his son George to read and study carefully the Word of God.

—Editor

St. Petersburg, Sept., 1811

My Dear Son:

In your letter of the 18th January to your mother, you mentioned that you read to your aunt a chapter in the Bible or a section of **Doddridge**'s *Annotations* every evening. This information gave me real pleasure; for so great is my veneration for the Bible, and so strong my belief, that when duly read and meditated on, it is of all books in the world, that which contributes most to make men good, wise, and happy. The earlier my children begin to read it, the more steadily they pursue the practice of reading it throughout their lives, the more lively and confident will be my hopes that they will prove useful citizens to their country, respectable members of society, and a real blessing to their par-

Philip Doddridge
JUNE 26, 1702 – OCTOBER 26, 1751

– GEORGE VERTUE

Remaining outside the Anglican Church as a Nonconformist, Rev. Philip Doddridge exercised one of the most remarkable Christian ministries of eighteen-century England. He distinguished himself as a leader, educator, and hymnwriter.

ents. But, I hope you have now arrived at an age to understand that reading—even in the Bible—is a thing in itself neither good nor bad, but that all the good which can be drawn from it is by the use and improvement of what you have read, with the help of your own reflection. Young people sometimes boast of how many books and how much they have read, when, instead of boasting, they ought to be ashamed of having wasted so much time to so little profit.

I advise you, my son, in whatever you read, and most of all in reading the Bible, to remember that it is for the purpose of making you wiser and more virtuous. I have myself, for many years, made it a practice to read through the Bible once every year. I have always endeavored to read it with the same spirit and temper of mind, which I now recommend to you. That is, with the intention and desire that it may contribute to my advancement in wisdom and virtue.

My desire is indeed very imperfectly successful, for, like you, and like the Apostle Paul, "I find a law in my members, warring against the laws of my mind." But, as I know that it is my nature to be imperfect, so I know that it is my duty to aim at perfection. And, feeling and deploring my own frailties, I can only pray Almighty God for the aid of his Spirit to strengthen my good desires and to subdue my propensities to evil, for it is from him that every good and every perfect gift descends. My custom is, to read four or five chapters every morning, immediately after rising from my bed. It employs about an hour of my time, and seems to me the most suitable manner of beginning the day. But, as other cares, duties, and occupations, engage the remainder of it, I have perhaps never a sufficient portion of my time in meditation, upon what I have read. Even meditation itself is often fruitless, unless it has some special object in view. Useful thoughts often arise in the mind, and pass away without being remembered or applied to any good purpose—like the seed scattered upon the surface of the ground, which the birds devour, or the wind blows away, or which rot without taking root—however good the soil may be upon which they are cast.

We are all, my dear George, unwilling to confess our own faults, even to ourselves. And, when our own consciences are too honest to conceal them from us, our self-love is always busy, either in attempting to disguise them to us under false and delusive colors, or in seeking out excuses and apologies to reconcile them to our minds. Thus, although I am sensible that I have not derived from my assiduous perusal of the Bible (and I might apply the same remark to almost everything else that I do) all the benefit that I might and ought, I am as constantly endeavoring to persuade myself that it is not my own fault. Sometimes I say to myself, I do not understand what I have read; I cannot help it; I did not make my own understanding.

There are many things in the Bible "hard to understand," as St. Peter expressly says of Paul's epistles. Some are hard in the Hebrew, and some in the Greek—the original languages in which the Scriptures were written; some are harder still in the translations. I have been obliged to lead a wandering life about the world, and scarcely ever have at hand the book, which might help me to surmount these difficulties. Conscience sometimes raises the question whether my not understanding many passages is not owing to my want of attention in reading them. I must admit, that it is. A full proof of which is that every time I read the Book through, I understand some passages which I never understood before, and which I should have done, at a former reading, had it been undertaken with a sufficient degree of attention.

Then, in answer to myself, I say, it is true; but I cannot always command my own attention, and never can to the degree that I wish. My mind is often so full of other things, absorbed in bodily pain, or engrossed by passion, or distracted by pleasure, or exhausted by dissipation, that I cannot give to proper daily employment the attention which I gladly would, and which is absolutely necessary to make it "fruitful of good works." This acknowledgment of my weakness is just, but for how much of it I am still accountable to God, I hardly dare acknowledge to myself. Is it bodily pain? How often was that brought upon me by my own imprudence or folly? Was it passion? Heaven has given to every human being, the power of controlling his passions, and if he neglects or loses it, the fault is his own, and he must be answerable for it. Was it pleasure Why did I indulge it? Was it dissipation? This is the most inexcusable of all, for it must have been occasioned by my own thoughtlessness or irresolution. It is of no use to discover our own faults and infirmities, unless the discovery prompts us to amendment.

I have thought if in addition to the hour which I daily give to the reading of the Bible, I should also from time to time (and especially on the Sabbath) apply another hour occasionally to communicate to you the reflections that arise in my mind upon its perusal, it might not only tend to fix and promote my own attention to the excellent instructions of that sacred Book, but perhaps also assist your advancement in its knowledge and wisdom. At your age, it is probable that you have still greater difficulties to understand all that you read in the Bible, than I have at mine. And, if you have so much self-observation as your letters indicate, you will be sensible of as much want of attention, both voluntary and involuntary, as I here acknowledge in myself.

I intend, therefore, for the purpose of contributing to your improvement and my own to write you several letters in due time to follow this, in which I shall endeavor to show you how you may derive the most advantage to yourself from the perusal of the Scriptures. It is probable, when you receive these letters, you will not at first reading entirely understand them. If that should be the case, ask your grand-parents, or your uncle or aunt, to explain them. If you still find them too hard, put them on file, and lay them by for two or three years, after which read them again, and you will find them easy enough.

It is essential, my son, in order that you may go through life with comfort to yourself, and usefulness to your fellow-creatures, that you should form and adopt certain rules or principles, for the government of your own conduct and temper. Unless you have such rules and principles, there will be numberless occasions on which you will have no guide for your government but your passions. In your infancy and youth, you have been, and will be for some years, under the authority and control of your friends and instructors, but you must soon come to the age when you must govern yourself. You have already come to that age in many respects.

You know the difference between right and wrong, and you know some of your duties, and the obligations you are under, to become acquainted with them all. It is in the Bible you must learn them, and from the Bible how to practice them. Those duties are to God, to your fellow-creatures, and to yourself. "Thou shall love the Lord thy God, with all thy heart, and with all thy soul, and with all thy mind, and with all thy strength, and thy neighbor as thyself." On these two commandments, Jesus Christ expressly says, "hang all the law and the prophets." That is to say, the whole purpose of Divine Revelation is to inculcate them efficaciously upon the minds of men.

You will perceive that I have spoken of duties to *yourself*, distinct from those to God and to your fellow-creatures, while Jesus Christ speaks only of two commandments. The reason is, because Christ, and the commandments repeated by him, consider self-love as so implanted in the heart of every man by the law of his nature, that it requires no commandment to establish its influence over the heart; and so great do they know its power to be, that they demand no other measure for the love of our neighbor, than that which they know we shall have for ourselves. But from the love of God, and the love of our neighbor, result duties to ourselves as well as to them, and they are all to be learned in equal perfection by our searching the Scriptures.

Let us, then, search the Scriptures, and in order to pursue our inquiries with methodical order, let us consider the various sources of information, that we may draw from in this study. The Bible contains the revelation of the will of God. It contains the history of the creation of the world, and of mankind; and afterward the history of one peculiar nation, certainly the most extraordinary nation that has ever appeared upon the earth. It contains a system of religion, and of morality, which we may examine upon its own merits, independent of the sanction it receives from being the Word of God; and it contains a numerous collection of books, written at different ages of the world, by different authors, which we may survey as curious monuments of antiquity, and as literary compositions. In whatever light we regard it, whether with reference to revelation, to literature, to history, or to morality—it is an invaluable and inexhaustible mine of knowledge and virtue.

I shall number separately those letters that I mean to write you upon the subject of the Bible, and as, after they are finished, I shall perhaps ask you to read them all together, or to look over them again myself, you must keep them on separate file. I wish that hereafter they may be useful to your brothers and sisters, as well as to you. As you will receive them as a token of affection for you, during my absence, I pray that they may be worthy to read by them all with benefit to themselves, if it please God, that they should live to be able to understand them.

From your affectionate Father,
John Quincy Adams

LETTER TWO:

SCRIPTURE AS DIVINE REVELATION

In his second letter to his son George, Mr. Adams argues that human reasoning alone cannot apprehend the nature and will of God. Rather, God must disclose his will to mankind, and the repository of God's revelation of himself is found in the Bible. It may be noted that Mr. Adams was very conversant with the pagan Greco-Roman world—as noted by his citations of Greek and Roman authors—and was, therefore, able to pass judgement upon the religious limitations of those cultures.

—Editor

The first point of view in which I have invited you to consider the Bible is in the light of *Divine Revelation*. And what are we to understand by these terms. I intend as much as possible to avoid the field of controversy, which I am not well acquainted with, and for which I have little respect and still less inclination. My idea of the Bible as a *Divine Revelation*, is founded upon its practical use to mankind, and not upon metaphysical subtleties.

There are three points of doctrine, the belief of which, forms the foundation of all morality. The first is, the existence of a God; the second is the immortality of the human soul; and the third is, a future state of rewards and punishments. Suppose it possible for a man to disbelieve either of these articles of faith, and that man will have no conscience, he will have no other law than that of the tiger or the shark. The laws of man may bind him in chains, or may put him to death, but they never can make him wise, virtuous, or happy. It is possible to believe them all without believing that the Bible is a Divine revelation.

It is so obvious to every reasonable being, that he did not make himself and the world which he inhabits, could as little make itself, that the moment we begin to exercise the power of reflection, it seems impossible to escape the conviction that there is a Creator. It is equally evident that the Creator must be a spiritual, and not a material being; there is also a consciousness that the thinking part of our nature is not material, but spiritual—that it is not subject to the laws of matter, nor perishable with it. Hence arises the belief, that we have an immortal soul, and pursuing the train of thought which the visible creation and observation upon ourselves suggest, we must soon discover that the Creator must also be the Governor of the universe; that his wisdom, and his goodness, must be without bounds—that he is a righteous God, and loves righteousness—that mankind are bound by the laws of righteousness, and are accountable to him for their obedience to them in this life, according to their good or evil deeds. This completion of Divine justice must be reserved for another life.

The existence of a Creator, the immortality of the human soul, and a future state of retribution, are therefore so perfectly congenial to natural reason when once discovered—or rather it is so impossible for natural reason to disbelieve them—that it would seem the light of natural reason could alone suffice for their discovery, but the conclusion would not be correct. Human reason may be sufficient to get an obscure glimpse of these sacred and important truths, but it cannot discover them, in all their clearness. For example, in all their numberless, false religions, which have swayed the minds of men in different ages, and regions of the world, the idea of a God has always been included:

"Father of all! in every age,
In every clime adored—
By saint, by savage, and by sage—
Jehovah, Jove, or Lord."

Alexander Pope
MAY 21, 1688 - MAY 30, 1744

— GODFREY KNELLER

A well-known 18th-century English poet, whose most famous religious poem was, *Essay on Man*. This poem was intended to be his centerpiece of a system of ethics.

So says Pope's *Universal Prayer*.[4] But, it is the God of the Hebrews alone, who is announced to us as the Creator of the world. The ideas of God entertained by all the most illustrious and most ingenious nations of antiquity were weak and absurd. The Persians worshipped the sun. The Egyptians believed in an innumerable multitude of gods, and worshipped not only oxen, crocodiles, dogs, and cats, but even garlics and onions. The Greeks invented a poetical religion, and adored men and women, virtues and vices, air, water, and fire, and everything that a vivid imagination could personify. Almost all the Greek

Marcus Tullius Cicero
JANUARY 3, 106 – DECEMBER 7 43 BC

— PALAZZO NUOVO

Cicero was a Roman politician and lawyer and was regarded as one of Rome's greatest orators and literary figures.

philosophers reasoned and meditated upon the nature of the

gods, but scarcely any of them reflected enough even to imagine that there was but one God, and not one of them ever conceived of him as the Creator of the world. **Cicero** has collected together all their opinions upon the nature of the gods, and pronounced them more like the dreams of madmen than the sober judgment of wise men. In the first book of **Ovid**'s *Metamorphoses*, there is an account of the change of chaos in the world. Before the sea, and the earth, and the sky that surrounds all things (says Ovid), there was a thing called chaos, and some of the gods (he does not know which), separated from each other the elements of this chaos, and turned them into the world; thus far and no farther could human reason extend.

Publius Ovidius Naso

MARCH 20, 43 BC – AD 17/18

– ETTORE FERRARI

Ovid was a Roman poet who lived during the reign of Augustus. Along with Virgil and Horace, Ovid was regarded as one of the most esteemed of Roman poets.

But the first words of the Bible are, "In the beginning God created the heavens and the earth." The blessed and sublime idea of God, as the creator of the universe, the source of all human happiness for which all the sages and philosophers of Greece and Rome groped in darkness and never found, is recalled in the first verse of the book of Genesis. I call it the source of all human virtue and happiness, because when we have attained the conception of a Being, who by the mere act of his will, created the world, it would follow as an irresistible consequence—even if we were not told that the same Being must also be the governor of his own creation—that man, with all other things, was also created by him, and must hold his felicity and virtue on the condition of obedience to his will. In the first chapters of the Bible, there is a short and rapid historical narrative of the manner in which the world and man were made—of the condition upon which happiness and immortality were bestowed upon our first parents—of their transgression of this condition—of the punishment denounced upon them-and the promise of redemption from it by the "seed of the woman."

There are, and always have been, where the Holy Scriptures have been known, petty witlings and self-conceited reasoners, who make petty objections to some of the particular details of this narration. Even serious inquirers after truth have sometimes been perplexed to believe that there should have been evening and morning before the existence of the sun; that man should be made of clay, and woman from the ribs of man; that they should have been forbidden to eat an apple, and for disobedience to that injunction, be with all their posterity doomed to death, and that eating an apple could give "the knowledge of good and evil"; and that a serpent should speak and beguile a woman. All this is undoubtedly marvelous, and above our comprehension. Much of it is clearly figurative and allegorical, nor is it easy to distinguish what part of it is to be understood in a literal and not in a symbolical sense.

> What Mr. Adams understands to be symbolic or figurative is not evident from his discussion, here, or elsewhere in his letters. What is important to remember, however, is the literal interpretation that the New Testament places upon much of the opening chapters of Genesis.

But, all that it imports us to know or understand is plain. The great and essential principles upon which our duties and enjoyments depend are involved in no obscurity. A God, the Creator and Governor of the universe, is revealed in all his majesty and power. The terms upon which he gave existence and happiness to the common parent of mankind are exposed to us in the clearest light. Disobedience to the will of God was the offence for which he was removed from paradise. Obedience to the will of God is the merit by which paradise is to be regained. Here, then, is the foundation of all morality—the source of all our obligations, as accountable creatures.

This idea of the transcendent power of the Supreme Being is essentially connected with that by which the whole duty of man is summed up—obedience to his will. I have observed that natural reason might suffice for an obscure perception, but not for the clear discovery of these truths. Even Cicero could entertain to his own mind the question, whether justice could exist upon earth unless founded upon fidelity to God, but could not settle it to his own satisfaction. The ray of divine light contained in the principle, that justice has no other foundation than fidelity to God, could make its way to the soul of the heathen, but there it was extinguished in, the low, unsettled, and inconsistent notions which were the only foundations of his fidelity to God. How could his fidelity to God be pure or sound, when he did not know whether there was one God or a thousand—whether he, or they had or had not any concern in the formation of the world, and whether they had any regard to the affairs or the conduct of mankind? Once the idea of a single God is assumed—the Creator of all things, whose will is the law of moral obligation to man, and to whom man is accountable, and fidelity to God becomes as rational as it is essential—it becomes the first of human duties, and not a doubt can henceforth remain that fidelity in the associations of human faithfulness, and that most excellent virtue, justice, rest upon no other foundation.

At a later age than Cicero, Longinus expressly quotes the third verse of the first chapter of Genesis as an example of the sublime. "And God said let there be light," and there was light and wherein consists its sublimity? In the image of the transcendent power presented to the mind, with the most striking simplicity of expression. Yet this verse only exhibits the effects of that transcendent power which the first verse discloses in announcing God as the Creator of the world. The true sublimity is in the idea given us of God. To such a God the heart of man must yield with cheerfulness the tribute of homage which it never could pay to the numerous gods of Egypt, to the dissolute debauchees of the heathen mythology, nor even to the more elevated, but not less fantastical imaginations of the Greek philosophers and sages.

From your affectionate Father,
John Quincy Adams

LETTER THREE:
SCRIPTURE AS HISTORY

In the following chapter, Mr. Adams seeks to call his son's attention to the importance of biblical history—something that obtains its significance because it is a record of the unfolding of God's plan of salvation in human history. Therefore, prominent details related to the way in which God achieved this are of great importance to Mr. Adams. Contrasting the disobedience of Adam and Eve and the sorrow their sin brought on the human race, he shows how the obedience of Abraham resulted in the coming of Jesus Christ, the Savior of the world.

—Editor

The second general point of view in which I propose for you to consider the Bible to the end that it may "thoroughly furnish you unto all good works," is in the historical character.

To a man of liberal education, the study of history is not only useful and important, but altogether indispensable. And, with regard to the history contained in the Bible, the observation which Cicero makes respecting that of his own country is much more emphatically applicable, that "it is not so much praiseworthy to be acquainted with as it is shameful to be ignorant of it."

History, so far as it relates to the actions and adventures of men, may be divided into five different classes: first, the history of the world, otherwise called universal history; second, that of particular nations; third, that of particular institutions; fourth, that of single families; and fifth, that of individual men. The last two of these classes are generally distinguished by the name of memoirs and biography. All these classes of history are to be found in the Bible, and it may be worth your while to discriminate them one from another.

The universal history is short, and all contained in the first eleven chapters of Genesis, together with the first chapter of the first book of Chronicles, which is little more than a genealogical list of names; but it is of great importance, not only as it includes the history of the creation, of the fall of man, of the world before the Flood, and the flood by which the whole human race (except Noah and his family) were destroyed, but as it gives a very precise account of the time from the creation until the birth of Abraham. This is the foundation of ancient history, and in reading profane historians hereafter, I would advise you always to reflect upon their narratives with reference to it with respect to the chronology. A correct idea of this is so necessary to understand all history, ancient and modern, that I may hereafter write you something further concerning it. For the present, I shall only recommend to your particular attention the fifth and eleventh chapters of Genesis, and request you to cast up and write me the amount of the age of the world when Abraham was born.

The remainder of the book of Genesis, beginning at the twelfth chapter, is a history of one individual (Abraham) and his family during three generations of his descendants, after which the book of Exodus commences with the history of the same family, multiplied into a nation. This national and family history is continued through the books of the Old Testament until that of Job, which is of a peculiar character, differing in many particulars from every other part of the Scriptures. There is no other history in existence which can give so interesting and correct view of the rise and progress of human associations, as this account of

Abraham and his descendants, through all the changing circumstances to which individuals, families, and nations, are liable.

There is no other history where the origin of a whole nation is traced up to a single man, and where a connected train of events and a regular series of persons from generation to generation is preserved. As the history of a family, it is intimately connected with our religious principles and opinions, for it is the family from which (in his human character) Jesus Christ descended. It begins by relating the commands of God to Abraham, to abandon his country, his kindred, and his father's house, and to go to a land which he would show him.

This command was accompanied by two promises, from which and from their fulfilment, arose the differences which I have just noticed between the history of the Jews and that of every other nation. The first of these promises was that, "God would make Abraham a great nation, and bless him." The second, and incomparably the most important was that, "in him all the families of the earth should be blessed." This promise was made about two thousand years before the birth of Christ, and in him had its fulfilment. When Abraham, in obedience to the command of God, had gone into the land of Canaan, the Lord appeared unto him and made him a third promise, which was that he should give that land to a nation which should descend from him, as a possession: this was fulfilled between five and six hundred years afterward. In reading all the historical books of both the Old and the New Testament, as well as the books of the prophets, you should always bear in mind the reference which they have to these three promises of God to Abraham. All the history is no more than a narrative of the particular manner, and the detail of events by which those promises were fulfilled.

In the account of the creation and the fall of man, I have already remarked that the moral doctrine inculcated by the Bible is that the great consummation of all human virtue consists in obedience to the will of God. When we come hereafter to speak of the Bible in its ethical character, I shall endeavor to show you the intrinsic excellence of this principle, but I shall now only remark how strongly the principle itself is illustrated, first in the account of the fall, and next by the history of Abraham.

In the account of the creation, we are informed that God, after having made the world, created the first human pair, and "gave them dominion over every living thing that moveth upon the earth." He gave them also "every herb bearing seed, and the fruit of every tree for meat." And, all this we are told, "God saw was very good." Thus, the immediate possession of everything was given them, and its perpetual enjoyment secured to their descendants on condition of abstaining from the "fruit of the tree of knowledge of good and evil." It is altogether immaterial to my present remarks whether the narrative is to be understood in a literal or allegorical sense, as not only the *knowledge*, but the possession of created good was granted. The fruit of the tree could confer upon them no knowledge but that of evil, and the command was nothing more than to abstain from that knowledge—to forbear from rushing upon their own destruction.

It is not sufficient to say that this was a command in its own nature light and easy. It was a command to pursue the only law of their nature, to keep the happiness that had been heaped upon them without measure. But, observe—it contained the principle of *obedience*—it was assigned to them as a duty—and the heaviest of penalties was denounced upon its transgression. They were not to discuss the wisdom, or justice of this command; they were not to inquire why it had been required of them, nor could they have the slightest possible motive for the inquiry. Unqualified felicity and immortality were already theirs. Wretchedness and death were alone forbidden them, but placed within their reach as merely trials of their obedience. They violated the law; they forfeited their joy and immortality; they "brought into the world, death, and all our woe."

Here, then, is an extreme case in which the mere principle of obedience could be tried, and command to abstain from that from which every motive of reason and interest would have deterred had the command never been given—a command given in the easiest of all possible form, requiring not so much as an action of any kind, but merely forbearance. And its transgression was so severely punished, the only inference we can draw from it is that the most aggravated of all crimes, and that which includes in itself all others, is disobedience to the will of God.

Let us now consider how the principle of obedience is inculcated in the history of Abraham, by a case in the opposite extreme. God commanded Abraham to abandon forever his country, his kindred, and his father's house, to go, he knew not where. God promised, as a reward of his obedience, to bless him and his posterity, though he was then childless. He was required to renounce everything that could most contribute to the happiness and comfort of his life, and which was in his actual enjoyment, to become a houseless, friendless wanderer upon the earth, on the mere faith of the promise that a land should be shown him which his descendants should possess— that they should be a great nation—and that through them all mankind should receive in future ages a blessing.

The obedience required of Adam, was merely to retain all the blessings he enjoyed. The obedience of Abraham was to sacrifice all that he possessed for the vague and distant prospect of a future compensation to his posterity. The self-control and self-denial required of Adam, was in itself the slightest that imagination can conceive—but its failure was punished by the forfeiture of all his enjoyments. The self-dominion to be exercised by Abraham was of the most severe and painful kind—but its accomplishment will ultimately be rewarded by the restoration of all that was forfeited by Adam. This restoration, however, was to be obtained by no ordinary proof of obedience.

The sacrifice of mere personal blessings, however great, could not lay the foundation for the redemption of mankind from death. The voluntary submission of Jesus Christ to his own death, in the most excruciating and ignominious form, was to consummate the great plan of redemption, but the submission of Abraham to sacrifice his beloved, and only son Isaac—the child promised by God himself, and through whom all the greater promises were to be carried into effect, the feelings of nature, the parent's bowels, were all required to be sacrificed by Abraham to the blind unquestioning principle of obedience to the will of God. The blood of Isaac was not indeed shed— the butchery of an only son by the hand of his father, was a sacrifice which a merciful God did not require to be completely executed, but as an instance of obedience it was imposed upon Abraham, and nothing less than the voice of an angel from heaven could arrest his uplifted arm, and withhold him from sheathing his knife in the heart of his child. It was upon this testimonial of obedience, that God's promise of redemption was expressly renewed to Abraham: "In thy seed shall all the nations of the earth be blessed, because thou hast obeyed my voice."—Genesis 22:18.

LETTER FOUR:
SCRIPTURE AS HISTORY—CONTINUED

For Mr. Adams, God's plan of redemption is the single thread that weaves together the tapestry of all biblical history. Comparing the disobedience of Adam with the obedience of Abraham, Mr. Adams outlines how Adam's disobedience brought sorrow to the world while Abraham's obedience resulted in the coming of the Messiah, Jesus Christ.

—Editor

We were considering the Bible in its historical character, and as the history of a family. From the moment when the universal history finishes, that of Abraham begins, and thenceforth, it is the history of a family, of which Abraham is the first, and Jesus Christ the last person. And, from the first appearance of Abraham, the whole history appears to have been ordered from age to age, expressly to prepare for the appearance of Christ upon earth. The history begins with the first and mildest trials of Abraham's obedience, and the promise as a reward of his faithfulness, that "in him all the families of the earth should be blessed." The second trial, which required the sacrifice of his son, was many years afterward, and the promise was more explicit, and more precisely assigned as the reward of his *obedience*.

There were between these periods, two intermediate occasions, recorded in the fifteenth and eighteenth chapters of Genesis— on the first of which, the word of the Lord came to Abraham in a vision, and promised him he should have a child, from whom a great and mighty nation should proceed, which, after being in servitude four hundred years in a strange land, should become the possessors of the land of Canaan, from that of Egypt, to the river Euphrates. On the second, the Lord appeared to him and his wife, repeated the promise, that they should have a child, that "Abraham should surely become a great nation," and that "all the nations of the earth should be blessed in him," "for I know him, saith the Lord, that he will command his household after him, and that they will keep the way of the Lord, to do justice and judgment, that the Lord may bring upon Abraham that which he hath spoken of him from all which it is obvious that the first of the promises was made as subservient and instrumental to the second—that the great and mighty nation was to be raised as the means in the ways of God's providence, for producing the sacred person of Jesus Christ, through whom the perfect sacrifice of atonement for the original transgression of man should be consummated, and by which "all the families of the earth should be blessed."

I am so little versed in controversial divinity, that I know not whether this eighteenth chapter of Genesis, has ever been adduced in support of the doctrine of Trinity. There is at least in it an alteration of those divine persons, and of one not a little remarkable which I know not how to explain. If taken in connection with the nineteenth, it would seem that one of the men entertained by Abraham, was God himself, and the other two were angels, sent to destroy Sodom.

Leaving this, however, let me call your attention, to the reason assigned by God for bestowing such extraordinary blessings upon Abraham. It unfolds to us the first and most important part of the superstructure of moral principle, erected upon the foundation of obedience to the will of God. The rigorous trials of Abraham's obedience mentioned in this, and my last letter, were only tests to ascertain his character in reference to the single, and I may say abstract point of obedience. Here we have a precious gleam of light, disclosing what the nature of this will of God was, that he should command his children, and his household after him, by which the parental authority to instruct, and direct his descendants in the way of the Lord was given him as an authority, and enjoined upon him as a duty. And, the lessons which he was then empowered and required to teach his posterity were, "to do justice and judgment." Thus, as obedience to the will of God, is the first, and all-comprehensive virtue taught in the Bible, so the second is justice and judgment toward mankind, and this is exhibited as the result naturally following from the other. In the same chapter is related the intercession of Abraham with God for the preservation of Sodom from destruction. The city was destroyed for its crimes, but the Lord promised Abraham it should be spared, if only ten righteous should be found in it. The principle of mercy was, therefore, sanctioned in immediate connection with that of justice.

Abraham had several children, but the great promise of God was to be performed through Isaac alone, and of the two sons of Isaac, Jacob—the youngest—was selected for the foundation of the second family and nation. It was from Jacob that the multiplication of the family began, and his twelve sons, were all included in the genealogy of the tribes which afterward constituted the Jewish people. Ishmael, the children of Keturah, and Esau, the eldest son of Isaac, were all the parents of considerable families, which afterward spread into nations. But, they formed no part of the chosen people, and their history with that of the neighboring nations is only incidentally noticed in the Bible, so far as they had relations of business or hostility with the people of God.

28

The history of Abraham and his descendants to the close of the book of Genesis is a biography of individuals. The incidents related of them are all of the class belonging to domestic life. Joseph, indeed, became a highly distinguished public character in the land of Egypt, and it was through him that his father and all his brothers were finally settled there—which was necessary to prepare for the existence of their posterity as a nation, and to fulfil the purpose which God had announced to Abraham, that they should be four hundred years dwellers in a strange land. In the lives of Abraham, Isaac, Jacob, and Joseph, many miraculous events are recorded, but all those which are spoken of as happening in the ordinary course of human affairs have an air of reality about them which no invention could imitate.

In some of the transactions related, the conduct of the patriarchs is highly worthy of blame. Circumstances of deep depravity are particularly told of Reuben, Simeon, Levi, and Judah, upon which it is necessary to remark that their actions are never spoken of with approbation, but always with strong marks of censure, and generally with a minute account of the punishment which followed upon their transgression. The vices and crimes of the patriarchs, are sometimes alleged as objections against the belief that persons guilty of them should ever have been especially favored by God, but, vicious as they were, there is every reason to be convinced that they were less so than their contemporaries. Their vices appear to us at this day gross, disgusting and atrocious, but the written law was not then given, the boundaries between right and wrong were not defined with the same precision as in the tables given afterward to Moses. The law of nature was the only rule of morality by which they could be governed, and the sins of intemperance, of every kind recorded in Holy Writ, were at that period less aggravated than they have been in after ages, because they were in great measure sins of ignorance.

From the time when the sons of Jacob were settled in Egypt until the completion of the four hundred years, during which God had foretold to Abraham that his family should dwell there, there is a chasm in the sacred history. We are expressly told that all the house of Jacob which came into Egypt, were threescore and ten. It is said then that Joseph died, as did all that generation, after which nothing further is related of their posterity than that "they were faithful and multiplied abundantly, and waxed exceeding mighty, and the land was filled with them, until there arose a new king who knew not Joseph." Upon arriving in Egypt, Jacob had obtained a grant from Pharaoh of the land of Goshen, a place particularly suited to the pasturage of flocks. Jacob and his family were shepherds, and this circumstance was, in the first instance, the occasion upon which that separate spot was assigned to them, and, secondarily, was the means provided by God for keeping separate two nations then residing together. Every shepherd was an abomination to the Egyptians, and the Israelites were shepherds, although dwelling in the land of Egypt. Therefore, the Israelites were sojourners and strangers, and by mutual antipathy toward each other, originating in their respective conditions, they were prevented from intermingling by marriage, and losing their distinctive character.

This was the cause which had been reserved by the Supreme Creator, during the space of three generations and more than four centuries, as the occasion for eventually bringing them out of the land, for in proportion as they multiplied, it had the tendency to excite the jealousies and fears of the Egyptian king—as actually happened. These jealousies and fears suggested to him a policy of the most intolerable oppression and the most severe cruelty toward the Israelites. Not contented with reducing them to the most degraded condition of slavery, and making their lives bitter with hard bondage, he conceived the project of destroying the whole race, by ordering all the male children to be murdered as soon as they were born. In the wisdom of Providence, this very command was the means of preparing this family—when they had multiplied into a nation—for their release from Egypt, and for their conquest of the land which had been promised to Abraham. And, it was at the same time the means of raising up the great warrior, legislator, and prophet, who was to be their deliverer and leader. From that point forward, they are to be considered as a people, and their history as that of a nation.

During a period of more than a thousand years, the Bible gives us a particular account of their experiences. An outline of their constitution, civil, military, and religious life, with the code of laws presented to them by God, is contained in the books of Moses, and will afford us abundant materials for future consideration. Their subsequent changes of government under Joshua, fifteen successive chiefs denominated judges, and a succession of kings, until they were first dismembered into two separate kingdoms, and after a lapse of some centuries both conquered by the Assyrians and Babylonians, and at the end of seventy years partially restored to their country and their temple, constitute the remaining historical books of the Old Testament, every part of which is full of instruction. But my present purpose is only to point your attention to their general historical character. My next will contain a few remarks on the Bible as a system of morals. In the meantime,

I remain your affectionate Father,
John Quincy Adams.

LETTER FIVE:
REVELATION AND RIGHTEOUSNESS

More than a year in time had elapsed between the previous letter (Letter Four) and the present letter. In his first paragraph, Mr. Adams explains that his perceived inability to fully comprehend and discuss the subject he wished to address has been his reason for not having written earlier. In this letter, Mr. Adams attempts to demonstrate how the Bible has produced a superior system of morality.

—Editor

At the conclusion of my last letter to you on the Bible, I undertook a task which I have previously been hindered by its very magnitude and importance. The more I reflected upon the subject, the more incompetent I felt to do it justice, and because of an all-to-common perception of inability to accomplish as much as I ought, I have prior to this point in time been held back from the attempt to accomplish anything at all. Thus, more than a year has elapsed, leaving me still burdened with the obligation of my promise, and in now undertaking to fulfil it, I must promise that you are only to expect the unorganized and undigested thoughts which I am incapable of combining into a regular and systematic work.

I shall not entangle myself in the controversy which has sometimes been discussed with a temper not very congenial to either the nature of the question itself or the undoubted principles of Christianity, whether the Bible, like all other systems of morality, lays the ultimate basis of all human duties in *self-love*, or whether it commands duties on the principle of *perfect*, and *disinterested benevolence*. Whether the obligations are sanctioned by a promise of reward or a menace of punishment, the ultimate motive for its fulfilment may justly be attributed to selfish considerations. But, if obedience to the will of God be the universal and only foundation of all moral duty, special injunctions may be binding upon the consciences of men, although their performance should not be secured either by the impulse of hope or fear.

The law given from Sinai was a civil and municipal as well as a moral and religious code. It contained many statutes adapted to that time only, and to the particular circumstances of the nation to whom it was given. They could of course be binding upon them, and only upon them, until set aside by the same authority which enacted them, as they afterward were by the Christian dispensation. But, many others were to be applied to all—laws essential to the existence of men in society, and most of which have been enacted by every nation, which ever professed any code of laws. But, the Levitical code was given by God himself. It extended to a great variety of objects of infinite importance to the welfare of men, but which could not come within the reach of human legislation. It combined the temporal and spiritual authorities together, and regulated not only the actions but the passions of those to whom it was given.

Human legislators can undertake only to prescribe the actions of men. They acknowledge their inability to govern and direct the sentiments of the heart. The very law designates it a rule of civil conduct, not principles of the heart; and, there is no crime in the power of an individual to perpetrate which he may not purpose, project, and fully intend, without incurring guilt in the eye of human law. It is one of the greatest marks of Divine favor bestowed upon the children of Israel, that the legislator gave them rules not only of action, but for the government of the heart. There were occasionally a few short sententious principles of morality issued from the oracles of Greece. Among them, and undoubtedly the most excellent of them, was that of self-knowledge, which one of the purest moralists and finest poets of Rome expressly says came from heaven.

But, if you would observe the distinguishing characteristics between true and false religion, compare the manner in which the Ten Commandments were proclaimed by the voice of the Almighty God, from Mount Sinai, with thunder, and lightning, and earthquake, by the sound of the trumpet, and in the presence of six thousand souls, with the deliberate secrecy, and mystery, and ridiculous ceremonies with which the Delphic and other oracles of the Greek gods were delivered. The miraculous display of Divine power recorded in every part of the Bible, are invariably marked with grandeur and sublimity worthy of the Creator of the world, and before which the gods of Homer, not excepting his Jupiter, dwindle into the most contemptible pigmies; but on no occasion was the manifestation of the Deity so solemn, so awful, so calculated to make indelible impressions upon the imaginations and souls of the mortals to whom he revealed himself, as when he appeared in the character of their

Lawgiver.

The law thus dispensed was, however, imperfect; it was destined to be partly suspended and improved into absolute perfection many ages afterward by the appearance of Jesus Christ upon earth. But to judge of its excellence as a system of laws, it must be compared with human codes which existed or were promulgated at nearly the same age of the world in other nations. Remember, that the law was given 1,490 years before Christ was born, at the time the Assyrian and Egyptian monarchies existed; but, of their government and laws we know scarcely anything except what is collected from the Bible. Of the Phrygian, Lydian, and Trojan states, at the same period, little more is known. President Goguet, in a very elaborate and ingenious work on the origin of letters, arts, and sciences, among the ancient nations, says, that "the maxims, the civil and political laws of these people, are absolutely unknown; that not even an idea of them can be formed, with the single exception of the Lydians, of whom Herodotus asserts, that their laws were the same as the Greeks."[5] The same author contrasts the total darkness and oblivion into which all the institutions of these mighty empires have fallen, with the fullness and clearness and admirable composition of the Hebrew code, which has not only descended to us entire, but still continues the national code of the Jews (scattered as they are over the whole face of the earth), and enters so largely into the legislation of almost every civilized nation upon the globe. He observes that "these laws have been prescribed by God himself: the merely human laws of other contemporary nations cannot bear any comparison with them."

But my motive in forming the comparison, is to present to your reflections as a proof—and to my mind a very strong proof—of the reality of their divine origin; for how is it that the whole system of government, and administration, the municipal, political, ecclesiastical, military, and moral laws and institutions, which bound in society the numberless myriads of human beings who formed for many successive ages the stupendous monarchies of Africa and Asia, should have perished entirely and been obliterated from the memory of mankind, while the laws

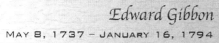

Edward Gibbon

MAY 8, 1737 – JANUARY 16, 1794

– JOSHUA REYNOLDS

Gibbon was an English historian, writer, and Member of Parliament. His most distinguished work was, The History of the Decline and Fall of the Roman Empire and is often remembered for his attacks upon Christianity and religion.

of a paltry tribe of shepherds, characterized by Tacitus, and the sneering infidelity of **Gibbon**, as "the most despised portion of their slaves," should not only have survived the wreck of those empires, but remain to this day rules of faith and practice to every enlightened nation of the world, and perishable only with it? The reason is obvious; it is their intrinsic excellence which has preserved them from the destruction which befalls all the works

Decalogue (dekə,lôg, 'dekə,läg)
noun (usually the Decalogue) the Ten Commandments.

of mortal man. The precepts of the Decalogue alone (says Goguet), disclose more sublime truths, more maxims essentially suited to the happiness of man, than all the writings of profane antiquity put together can furnish. The more you meditate on the laws of Moses, the more striking and brighter does their wisdom appear. It would be a laborious but not an unprofitable investigation, to reduce into a regular classification, like that of the institutes of Justinian or the Commentaries of Blackstone,

William Blackstone
JULY 1 0, 1 7 2 3 – FEBRUARY 1 4, 1 7 8 0

– UNKNOWN ARTIST

Blackstone was one of the most widely known and highly respected of jurists and judges in England. His *Commentaries on the Laws of England* were not only highly regarded in England, but were used in America for generations.

the whole code of Moses, which embraces not only all the ordinary subjects of legislation together with the principles of religion and morality, but laws of ecclesiastical directions concerning the minutest actions and dress of individuals. This, however, would lead me too far from my present purpose, which is merely to consider the Bible as a system of morality; I shall therefore notice those parts of the law which may be referred particularly to that class, and at present must confine myself to a few remarks upon the Decalogue itself, which, having been spoken by the voice, and twice written upon the stone tables by the finger of God, may be considered as the foundation of the whole system-of the Ten Commandments, emphatically so called, for the extraordinary and miraculous distinction by which they were put into effect.

The first four commandments are religious laws, the fifth and tenth are properly and peculiarly moral and domestic rules. The other four are of the criminal department of municipal laws. The unity of the godhead, the prohibition of making graven images to worship, that of taking lightly (or in vain as the English translation expresses it) the name of the Deity, and the injunction to observe the Sabbath as a day sanctified and set apart for his worship, were all intended to inculcate the reverence for the one only and true God—that profound and penetrating sentiment of fidelity to God which, in a former letter, I urged as the great and only immovable foundation of all human virtue. Next to the duties toward the Creator, that of honoring the earthly parent is enjoined. It is to them that every individual owes the greatest obligations, and to them that he is consequently bound by the first and strongest of all earthly ties.

The following commands, applying to the relations between man and his fellow mortals, are all negative, as their application was universal—to every human being. It was not required that any positive acts of generosity toward them should be performed, but only to abstain from harming them—either first, by harming their persons; or second, their property; or third, their marital rights; or fourth, their good name. After which, all the essential enjoyments of life being thus guarded from voluntary injury, the tenth and closing commandment goes to the very source of all human actions—the heart—and positively forbids all those desires which first prompt and lead to every transgression upon the property and right of our fellow-creatures.

Vain, indeed, would be the search among the writings of profane antiquity (not merely of that remote antiquity, but even in the most refined and philosophical ages of Greece and Rome), to find so broad, so complete and so solid a basis for morality as this Decalogue lays down. Yet, I have said it was imperfect— its sanctions, its rewards, its punishments, had reference only to present life, and it had no injunctions of positive beneficence toward our neighbors. Of these the law was not entirely destitute in its other parts; but, both in this respect and in the other, it was to be perfected by him who brought life and immortality to light in the gospel, upon which subject you shall hear more.

From your affectionate Father,
John Quincy Adams.

LETTER SIX:
REVELATION AND RIGHTEOUSNESS—CONTINUED

For Mr. Adams, the key to right living was right revelation. That is, he believed it was necessary to have a right understanding of God if an individual was to enjoy a right understanding of living. For this reason, he argues for the purity and uniqueness of Scripture as compared to the pagan world. Believing the Bible provided a correct image of God, Mr. Adams believed its teachings of morality could produce the highest form of righteousness.

—Editor

I promised you, in my last letters, to state the particulars in which I deemed the Christian dispensation to be an improvement, or perfection of the law delivered at Sinai, considered as including a system of morality. But, before I come to this point, it is proper to remark upon the character of the books of the Old Testament which follow those of **Moses**. Some are historical,

> There are five books that are regarded as the "Books of Moses" (also called the Pentateuch). They are Genesis, Exodus, Leviticus, Numbers and Deuteronomy.

some prophetic, and some poetic. Two of which may be regarded particularly of the moral class—one being an affecting dissertation upon the vanity of human life, and another a collection of moral sentences under the name of Proverbs. I have already considered that the great immovable and eternal foundation of scripture morals are superior to all other forms of morality. The nature of God is disclosed in them and only in them; the unity of God, his omnipotence, his righteousness, his mercy, and the infinity of his attributes, are marked in every line of the Old Testament, in characters which nothing less than blindness, can fail to discern, and nothing less than fraud can misrepresent. This conception of God which served as a basis for the reverence of his worshippers, was of course incomparably more rational and more profound than was possible through the sentiment accorded to devils for deities. Even the philosophers, like Socrates, Plato, and Cicero—who with purer and more exalted ideas of the Divine nature than the rabble of the poets—still considered the existence of any God at all, as a question upon which they could form no final opinion. You have seen that even Cicero believed the only solid foundation of all human virtue to be fidelity to God; and it was impossible that a fidelity to God so far transcending that of all other nations should not contain in its consequences a system of moral virtue equally superior.

The first of the Ten Commandments was, that the Jewish people should never accept the idea of any other God—the object of the second, third, and fourth, was merely to impress with greater force the obligation of the first, and to obviate the tendencies and temptations, which might arise to its being neglected, or disregarded. Throughout the whole law, the same injunctions are continually renewed; all the rites and ceremonies were adapted to root deeper into the hearts and souls of the chosen people, that the Lord Jehovah was to be forever the sole and exclusive object of love. Reverence and adoration—unbounded just as his own nature—were the principles which to guide his worshipers. Every letter of the law, and the whole Bible is but a commentary upon it, and corollary from it.

The law was given not merely in the form of a commandment

from God, but in the form of a covenant or compact between the Supreme Creator and the Jewish people. It was sanctioned by the blessing and the curse pronounced upon Mount Gerizim and Mount Ebal, in the presence of the whole Jewish people and strangers, and by the solemn acceptance of the whole people responding amen to every one of the curses denounced for violation on their part of the covenant. From that day until the birth of Christ (a period of about fifteen hundred years) the historical books of the Old Testament, are no more than a simple record of the fulfilment of the covenant, in all its blessings and curses, exactly adapted to the fulfilment or transgression of its duties by the people. The nation was first governed by Joshua, under the express appointment of God. Then they were governed by a succession of judges, and afterward by a double line of kings until conquered and carried into captivity by the kings of Assyria and Babylon. Seventy years later, they were restored to their country, their temple, and their laws, and again conquered by the Romans, and ruled by their tributary kings and proconsuls. Yet, through all their vicissitudes of fortune, they never complied with the duties to which they had bound themselves by the covenant without being under the blessings promised on Mount Gerizim, and never departed from the duties without being afflicted with some of the curses denounced upon Mount Ebal.

The prophetical books are themselves historical—for prophecy, in the strictest sense, is no more than history related before the event. But, the Jewish prophets (of whom there was a succession almost constant, from the time of Joshua to that of Christ) were messengers, specially commissioned of God, to warn the people of their duty, to foretell the punishments which awaited their transgressions, and finally to keep alive by uninterrupted prediction the expectation of the Messiah, "the seed of Abraham, in whom all the families of the earth should be blessed."

With this conception of the Divine nature, so infinitely surpassing that of any other nation—with this system of moral virtue, so indissolubly blending as by the eternal constitution of things must be blended fidelity to God, with this uninterrupted series of signs and wonders, prophets and seers, miraculous intervention of the omnipotent Creator, to preserve and vindicate the truth—it is lamentable that the Jewish people failed to follow God's will. But, to those who know the nature of man, it is not surprising to find the Jewish history little else than a narrative of idolatries and corruption of the Israelites and their monarchs. That the very people who had heard the voice of God from Mount Sinai, within forty days compel Aaron to make a golden calf, and worship that as the "God who brought them out of the land of Egypt." Solomon, the wisest of mankind, to whom God had twice revealed himself in visions, the sublime dictator of the temple, the witness in the presence of the whole people of the fire from heaven which consumed the offerings from the altar and of the glory of the Lord that filled the Temple that he— in his old age was beguiled by fair idolatresses—should have fallen from the worship of the ever-blessed Jehovah, to that of Ashtaroth and Milcom, etc. And, the abomination of all the petty tribes of Judea is no less remarkable, who followed after Baal, and Dagon, etc., the sun, moon, and planets, and all the host of heaven—that the mountains and plains, every high place and every grove, swarmed with idols, to corrupt the hearts and debase the minds of a people so highly favored of Heaven. The elect of the Almighty may be among the mysteries of Divine providence, which it is not given to mortality to explain, but is inadmissible only to those who presume to demand why it has pleased the Supreme Arbiter of events, to create such a being as man.

Observe, however, that amid the atrocious crimes which that nation so often polluted themselves with—through all their enslavements, dismemberments, captivities, and transmigrations—the Divine light, which had been imparted exclusively to them, was never extinguished. The law delivered from Sinai, was preserved in all purity. The histories which attested its violations and its accomplishments were recorded and never lost. The writings of the prophets, of David, and Solomon, were all inspired with the same idea of the Godhead, the same inter-twinement of religion and morality, and the same anticipations of the divine "Immanuel, the God with us." These survived all the changes of government and of constitutions which befell the people, similar to the abiding presence of God symbolized by "the pillar of cloud by day, and the pillar of fire by night." The law and the prophets—eternal in their nature—went before them unsullied, and unimpaired through all the ruins of rebellion and revolution, of conquest and dispersion, of war, pestilence, and famine.

The Assyrian, Babylonian, and Egyptian empires, Tyre and Sidon, Carthage, and all the other nations of antiquity, rose and fell in their religious institutions at the same time as in their laws and government. It was the practice of the Romans, when they besieged a city, to invoke its gods to come over to them. They considered the gods as summer friends, ready to desert their worshippers in the hour of calamity, or as traitors, ready to sell themselves for a bribe. They had no higher estimate of their own than of the stranger deities, whom, as Gibbon said, "they were always ready to admit to the freedom of the city." All the gods of the heathens have perished with their makers; for where on the face of the globe, could now be found the being who believes in any one of them?

So much more deep and strong was the hold which the God of Abraham, Isaac, and Jacob, took upon the imaginations and reason of mankind, that I might almost invert the question,

a·poc·ry·phal (əˈpäkrəfəl)

adjective; (of a story or statement) of doubtful authenticity, although widely circulated as being true.

In some versions of the OT, there appear fourteen extra books. These books are known as the Apocrypha, meaning "hidden away." These books were probably written between 200 B.C. and 100 A.D., though the exact date is difficult to determine. It seems that Jerome was the first to designate these books as the Apocrypha.

and say, "Where is the human being found believing in any God at all, and not believing in him?"

The moral character of the Old Testament, then, is, that fidelity to God is the foundation of all virtue, and that virtue is inseparable from it. But, that fidelity to God without the practice of virtue is itself a crime and the aggravation of all iniquity. All the virtues which are here recognized by the heathen, are inculcated not only with more authority but with more energy of argument and more eloquent persuasion in the Bible than in all the writings of the ancient moralists. In one of the **_apocryphal books_** (Wisdom of Solomon), the cardinal virtues are expressly named: "If any man love righteousness, her labors are virtue, for she teacheth temperance, and prudence, and justice, and fortitude," which are such things as men can have nothing more profitable in this life. The book of Job, whether considered as history or as an allegorical parable, was written to teach the lessons of patience under afflictions, of resignation under Divine chastisement, of undoubted confidence in the justice and goodness of God under every temptation or provocation to depart from it.

The morality of the apocryphal books is generally the same as that of the inspired writers, except that in some of them there is more stress laid upon the minor objects of the law, and merely formal ordinances of police, and less continual recurrence to "the weightier matters." The book of Ecclesiasticus, however, contains more wisdom than all the sayings of the seven Greek sages. It was upon this foundation that the more perfect system of Christian morality was to be raised. But I must defer the consideration to my next letter.

In the meantime as I have urged that the scriptural idea of God is the foundation of all perfect virtue, and that it is totally different from the idea of God conceived by any ancient nation, I should recommend it to you in pursuing the Scriptures hereafter to meditate often upon the expressions by which they mark the character of the Deity, and to reflect upon the duties to him and to your fellow mortals which follow by inevitable deductions from them. That you may have an exact idea of the opinions of ancient heathen philosophers concerning God, or rather the gods, study Cicero's dialogues, and read the able Olivet's remarks on the theology of the Greek philosophers, annexed to his translations.

From your affectionate Father,
John Quincy Adams

LETTER SEVEN:

PERFECT REVELATION BRINGS PERFECTION

In this letter, Mr. Adams asserts that Christ is the fullest revelation of God. As such, Christ discloses the nature of God and provides a means of moral life which he regards as a qualified "perfection." He argues that God's fullest revelation results in God's fullest expectation for the life of the believer.

—Editor

The imperfections of the Mosaic institution which it was the object of Christ's mission upon earth to remove, appear to me to have been these—First, the want of a sufficient sanction. The rewards and penalties of the Levitical law had all a reference to the present life. There are many passages in the Old Testament which imply a state of existence after death, and some which directly assert a future state of retribution; but, none of these were contained in the delivery of the law. At the time of Christ's advent, it was so far from being a settled article of the Jewish faith, that it was a subject of bitter controversy between the two principal sects—of Pharisees who believed in, and Sadducees who denied it. It was the special purpose of Christ's appearance upon earth, to bring immortality to light. He substituted the rewards and punishments of a future state of existence in the room of all others. The Jewish sanctions were exclusively temporal; those of Christ exclusively spiritual.

48

Second, the opportunity for universal observance of true religion was also needed. The Jewish dispensation was exclusively confined to a small and obscure nation. The purposes of the Supreme Creator in restricting the knowledge of himself to one petty herd of Egyptian slaves, are as inaccessible to our intelligence as those of his having concealed from them, and from the rest of mankind, the certain knowledge of their own immortality. Yet, the fact is unquestionable. The mission of Christ was intended to communicate to the whole human race all the permanent advantages of the Mosaic law, superadding to them—upon the condition of repentance—the kingdom of heaven, the blessing of eternal life.

Third, the complexity of the objects of legislation was not capable of being universal. I have observed in a former letter, that the law from Sinai comprised, not only all the ordinary subjects of regulation for human societies, but those which human legislators cannot reach. It was a civil law, a municipal law, an ecclesiastical law, a law of police, and a law of morality and religion. It prohibited murder, adultery, theft, and perjury, and it prescribed rules for the thoughts as well as for the actions of men. The complexity—however practicable and even suitable for one small national society—could not have attained to all the families of the earth. The parts of the Jewish law adapted to promote the happiness of mankind, under every variety of situation and government in which they can be placed, were all recognized and adopted by Christ, and he expressly separated them from the rest. He disclaimed all interference with the ordinary objects of human legislation, declared that his "kingdom was not of this world," acknowledged the authority of the Jewish magistrates, paid for his own person the tribute to the Romans, refused in more than one instance to assume the office of judge in matters of legal controversy, strictly limited the object of his own precepts and authority to religion and morals, denounced no temporal punishment, promised no temporal rewards, took up man as a governable being—where the human magistrate is compelled to leave him—and supplied both precept of virtue and motive for practicing it, such as no other moralist or legislator ever attempted to introduce.

Fourth, the burdensome duties of positive rites, minute formalities, and expensive sacrifices made the Mosaic Law impractical for universal observance. All these had a tendency, not only to establish and maintain the separation of the Jews from all other nations, but in process of time had been mistaken by the scribes, and Pharisees, and lawyers, and probably by the body of the people, for the substance of religion. All the rites were abolished by Christ, or (as Paul expresses it) "were nailed to his cross." You will recollect that I am now speaking of Christianity, not as the scheme of redemption to mankind from the consequences of original sin, but as a system of morality for regulating the conduct of men while on earth. And, the most striking and extraordinary feature of its character in this respect, is its tendency and exhortations to absolute perfection. The language of Christ to his disciples is explicit: "Be ye therefore perfect, even as your father in heaven is perfect"—and this he enjoins at the conclusion of that precept, so expressly laid down, and so unanswerably argued, to "love their enemies, to bless those who cursed them, and pray for those who despitefully used and persecuted them." He seems to consider the temper of love in return for injury, as constituting of itself a perfection similar to that of the Divine nature. It is undoubtedly the greatest conquest which the spirit of man can achieve over its infirmities, and to him who can attain that elevation of virtue which it requires, all other victories over the evil passions must be comparatively easy. Nor, was the absolute perfection merely preached by Christ as a doctrine. It was practiced by himself throughout his life; practiced to the last instant of his agony on the cross; practiced under circumstances of trial, such as no other human being was ever exposed to. He proved by his own example the possibility of that virtue which he taught, and although possessed of miraculous powers sufficient to control all the laws of nature, he expressly and repeatedly declined the use of them to save himself from any part of the sufferings which he was able to endure.

The sum of Christian morality, then, consists in fidelity to God, and love to man. Fidelity to God, manifested, not by formal, solemn rites and sacrifices of burnt-offerings, but by repentance, by obedience, by submission, by humility, by the worship of the heart, and by benevolence—not founded upon selfish motives, but superior even to a sense of wrong, or the resentment of injuries. Interest in worldly pursuits is scarcely noticed among all the instructions of Christ. The pursuit of honors and riches, the objects of ambition and avarice are strongly discountenanced in many places, and an undue solicitude about the ordinary cares of life is occasionally reproved. Of worldly prudence or pursuits, there are rules enough in the Proverbs of Solomon, and in the compilations of the son of Sirach. Christ passes no censure upon them, but he left what I call the selfish virtues where he found them. It was not to proclaim commonplace morality that he came down from Heaven. His commands were new—that his disciples should "love one another, " that they should love even strangers, that they should " love their enemies." He prescribed barriers against all the maleficent passions, and he gave as a law, the utmost point of perfection of which human powers are susceptible, and at the same time allowed degrees of indulgence and relaxation to human frailty,

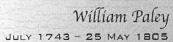

William Paley

JULY 1743 – 25 MAY 1805

– GEORGE ROMNEY

Paley was an English clergyman, Christian apologist, and philosopher. He is most widely remembered for his advocacy of natural theology, making use of the watchmaker analogy.

proportioned to the power of any individual. An eminent writer in support of Christianity (**Dr. Paley**) expresses the opinion, that the direct object of the Christian revelation was to supply *motives*, and not *rules—sanctions*, and not *precepts*; and he strongly intimates that, independent of the purpose of Christ's atonement and propitiation for the sins of the world, the only object of his mission upon earth was to reveal a future state, "to bring life and immortality to light." He does not appear to think that Christ promulgated any new principle of morality, and he positively asserts that "morality, neither in the gospel nor in any other book, can be a subject of discovery, because qualities of actions depend entirely on their effects, which effects, must all along have been the subjects of human experience." To this I reply in the express words of Jesus: "A new commandment I give you, that ye love one another;" and I add, that this command explained, illustrated, and expanded, as it was by the whole tenor of his discourses, and especially by the parable of the good Samaritan, appears to me to be not only entirely new, but, in the most rigorous sense of the word, a discovery in morals; and a discovery, the importance of which to the happiness of the human race, as far exceeds any discovery in the physical laws of nature, as the soul is superior to the body.

If someone objects, saying that the principles of love toward enemies and the forgiveness of injuries may be found not only in the Old Testament, but even in some of the heathen writers, particularly the discourses of Socrates, I answer, that the same may be said of the immortality of the soul, and of the rewards and punishments of a future state. The doctrine was not more a discovery than the precept; but their connection with each other, the authority with which they were taught, and the miracles by which they were enforced, belong exclusively to the mission of Christ.

Give particular attention to the miracle recorded in the second chapter of Luke, as having taken place as the birth of Jesus. When the angel of the Lord said to the shepherds, "Fear not, for behold I bring you glad tidings of great joy, which shall be to all people; for unto you is born this day in the city of David, a Savior, who is Christ the Lord." In these words, the character of

Jesus, as a Redeemer, was announced, but the historian adds, "And suddenly there was with the angel a multitude of the heavenly host praising God and singing, glory to God in the highest, and on earth peace, good will toward men." These words, as I understand them, announced the moral precept of love as explicitly for the object of Christ's appearance, as the preceding words had declared the purpose of redemption. It is related in the life of the Roman dramatic poet, Terence, that when one of the personages of his comedy, the "Self- Tormentor," the first time uttered on the stage the line "Homo sum, humani nil alienum puto" (I am a man, nothing human is uninteresting to me), a universal shout of applause burst forth from the whole audience, and that in so great a multitude of Romans, and deputies from the nations, their subjects and allies, there was not one individual but felt in his heart this noble sentiment.

Yet how feeble and defective it is, in comparison with the Christian command of love as unfolded in the discoveries of Christ and enlarged upon in the writings of his apostles. The heart of man will always respond with rapture to this sentiment when there is no selfish or unsocial passion to oppose it. But, the command to lay it down as the great and fundamental rule of conduct for human life, and to subdue and sacrifice all the tyrannical and selfish passions to preserve it, this is the peculiar and unfading glory of Christianity; this is the conquest over ourselves, which, without the aid of a merciful God, none of us can achieve, and which it was worthy of his special interposition to enable us to accomplish.

From your affectionate Father,
John Quincy Adams

LETTER EIGHT:

ASPIRING TO PERFECTION

*Likely influenced by the Methodists' teaching on Christian perfec-
tion, Mr. Adams encourages his son to seek a form of Christianity
that would embrace the most mature teachings of Jesus Christ. For
decades, any form of discussion concerning Christian perfection has
been derided and ridiculed by many late-twentieth and early-twenty-
first-century Christians. But, as Mr. Adam's discussion demon-
strates, this subject has always been part of Christian teaching in
the warmest eras of Christian revival and influence.*

—Editor

The whole system of Christianity appears to have been set forth
by its Divine Author in his sermon on the mount, recorded in
the fifth, sixth, and seventh chapters of Matthew. I intend hereafter to make them the subject of remarks much more at large;
for the present, I confine myself merely to general views. What
I would impress upon your mind, is infinitely important to the
happiness and virtue of your life, as the general spirit of Christianity, and the duties which results from it. In my last letter, I

showed you, from the very words of our Savior, that he commanded his disciples to aim at absolute perfection, and that this perfection consisted in self-subjugation and brotherly love, in the complete conquest of our own passions and in the practice of love to our fellow-creatures.

Among the Greek systems of moral philosophy, that of the Stoics resembles the Christian doctrine, particularly by requiring the total subjugation of the passions, and this part of the Stoic principles was adopted by the academies. You will find the question discussed with all the eloquence and ingenuity of Cicero, in the fourth of his Tusculan disputations, which I advise you to read and meditate upon. You will there find proved, the duty of subduing the passions.

It is sometimes objected that this theory is not adapted to the infirmities of human nature, that it is not made for a being so constituted as man, that an earthen vessel is not formed to dash itself against a rock, that in yielding to the impulses of the passions, man only follows the dictates of his nature, and that to subdue them entirely is an effort beyond his powers. The weakness and frailty of our nature, it is not possible to deny—it is too strongly tested by all human experience, as well as by the whole tenor of the Scriptures, but the degree of weakness must be measured by the efforts to overcome it, and not by indulgence to it. Once admit weakness as an argument to forbear exertion, and it results in absolute impotence. It is also very inconclusive reasoning to infer, that because perfection is not absolutely to be obtained, it is therefore not to be sought.

Human excellence consists in approximation to perfection, and the only means of approaching to any term, is by endeavoring to obtain the term itself. With these convictions upon the mind-with a sincere and honest effort to practice upon them, and with the aid of a divine blessing—which is promised to it—the approaches to perfection may at least be so great, as to nearly answer all the ends which absolute perfection itself could attain.

All exertion, therefore, is virtue, and if the tree be judged by its fruit, it is certain that all the most virtuous characters of heathen antiquity, were the disciples of the Stoic doctrine. But let it even be admitted that a perfect command of the passions is unattainable to human infirmity, it will still be true, that the degree of moral excellence possessed by any individual is in exact proportion to the degree of control he exercises over himself. According to the Stoics, all vice was resolvable into folly; according to the Christian principle it is all the effect of weakness. In order to preserve the dominion of our own passions, it behooves us to be constantly and strictly on our guard against the influence and infection of the passions of others.

This caution above all is necessary to youth, and I regard it indispensable to enjoin it upon you—because, as kindness and love comprise the whole system of Christian duties, there may be, and often is, great danger of falling into errors and vice, merely for the want of energy to resist the example or enticement of others. On this point the true character of Christian morality appears to me to have been misunderstood by some of its ablest and warmest defenders.

In Paley's, *View of the Evidences of Christianity*, there is a chapter upon the morality of the gospel, the general tenor, of which (as of the whole work) is excellent, but in which there is the following passage: "There are two opposite descriptions of character, under which mankind may generally be classed. The one possesses vigor, firmness, resolution, is active and daring, quick in its sensibilities, jealous of its fame, eager in its attachments, inflexible of its purposes, violent in its resentment; the other meek, yielding, complying, forgiving, not prompt to act, but willing to suffer, silent and gentle under rudeness and insults, suing for reconciliation, where others would demand satisfaction; giving away to the pushes of impudence, conceding and indulgent to the prejudices, the wrongheadedness, the intractability of others, with whom it has to deal. The former of these characters is, and ever has been, the favorite of the world; it is the character of great men—there is a dignity in it which commands respect. The latter is poor-spirited, tame, and abject. Yet, so it has happened, that with the founder of Christianity, the latter is the subject of his commendation, his precepts, his example, and that the former is so in no part of its composition." Dr. Paley, in this place adopts the opinion of Soame Jennings, whose essay on the *Internal Evidences of Christianity* he strongly recommends; but I cannot consider it either as an accurate and discerning delineation of character, nor as exhibiting a correct representation of Christian principles.

The founder of Christianity did indeed pronounce distinct and positive blessings upon the "poor in spirit"—which is by no means synonymous with the "poor-spirited"—and upon the meek; but in what part of the gospel did Dr. Paley find him countenancing by "commendation, by precept or example, the tame and abject"? The character which Christ assumed upon earth, was that of a Lord and Master. It was in that character his disciples received and acknowledged him. The obedience he required was unbounded, infinitely beyond that which was ever claimed by the most absolute earthly sovereign of his subjects. Never for one moment did he recede from this authoritative station. He preserved it in washing the feet of his disciples;

he preserved it in answer to the officer who struck him for this very deportment to the high-priest; he preserved it in the agony of his exclamation on the cross, "Father, forgive them, for they know not what they do." He expressly declared himself, "the Prince of this world, and the Son of God." He spoke as one having authority, not only to his disciples, but to his mother, to his judges, to Pilate the Roman governor, to John the Baptist— his precursor. And, there is not in the four gospels, one act, not one word recorded of him (excepting his communion with God) that was not a direct or implied assertion of authority. He said to his disciples, "Learn of me, for I am meek and lowly of heart," etc.; but where did he ever say to them, "Learn of me, for I am tame and abject"? There is certainly nothing more strongly marked in the precepts and examples of Christ, than the principle of stubborn and inflexible resistance against the impulses of others to evil. He taught his disciples to renounce everything that is counted enjoyment upon earth—"to take up their cross," and to suffer ill-treatment, persecution, and death, for his sake.

What else is the book of the "Acts of the Apostles," than a record of the faithfulness with which these chosen ministers of the gospel carried these injunctions into execution? In the conduct and speeches of Peter, John, and Paul, is there anything that could justly be called "tame or abject"? Is there anything indicating a resemblance to the second class of character into which Dr. Paley divides all mankind? If there is a character upon historical record distinguished by a bold, inflexible, tenacious, and intrepid spirit, it is that of Paul. It was to such characters only that the commission to "teach all nations" could be committed with certainty of success. Observe the impression of Christ, in his charge to Peter (a rock): "And upon this rock I will build my church, and the gates of hell shall not prevail against it."

Dr. Paley's Christian is one who speaks foolishly, who—to use a vulgar phrase—can never say no, to anybody. The true Christian is the "Justum et tenacem propositi virum" of Horace, ("the man who is just and steady to his purpose"). The combination of these qualities so essential to heroic character, with those of meekness, lowliness of heart, and brotherly love, is what constitutes that moral perfection of which Christ gave an example in his own life, and to which he commands his disciples to aspire.

Endeavor, my dear son, to discipline your heart and to govern your conduct by these principles thus combined. Be meek, be gentle, be kindly affectionate to all mankind—not excluding your enemies. But, never be "tame or abject;" never give way to the pushes of impudence, or show yourself yielding or complying to prejudice, wrong-headedness, or intractability, which would lead or draw you astray from the dictates of your own conscience, and your own sense of right: "till you die, let not your integrity depart from you." Build your house upon the rock, and then let the rains descend, and the floods come, and the winds blow and beat upon that house—"it shall not fall, it will be founded upon a rock."

So promises your blessed Lord and Master, and so prays your affectionate Father.

John Quincy Adams

LETTER NINE:
THE LITERARY COMPOSITION OF THE BIBLE

Delving into the ancient character of the Bible, Mr. Adams iden-
tifies its uniqueness. While avoiding an extended discussion of the
origin and transition of the Bible, he seeks to make several obser-
vations concerning the style of literature contained in Scripture.
Very likely Mr. Adams understood that the style of literature is
of great importance to a proper interpretation of the Bible, and for
this reason wished to apprise his son of this fact.

—Editor

The fourth and last point of view in which I proposed to offer
you some general observations upon the Scriptures was with
reference to literature, and the first remark that presents itself is
that the five books of Moses, are the most ancient monuments
of written language now existing in the world. The book of Job
is nearly of the same date and by many of the Jewish and Christian commentators is thought to have been written by Moses.
The employment of alphabetical characters to represent all the

articulations of the human voice is the greatest invention that ever was compassed by human genius. Plato says that, "it was the discovery of either a God, or a man divinely inspired." The Egyptians ascribed it to Thoth, whom the Greeks afterward worshipped under the name of Hermes. This is, however, a fabulous origin. That it was an Egyptian invention, there is little doubt; and it was a part of that learning of the Egyptians, in all of which we are told, "Moses was versed." It is probable that when Moses wrote, this act was—if not absolutely recent—of no very remote invention.

There was but one copy of the law written in a book. It was deposited in the ark of the covenant and was read aloud once in seven years to all the people, at their general assembly in the feast of tabernacles. There was one other copy of the law, written upon stone, erected on Mount Ebal. It does not appear that there existed any other copies. In process of time the usage of reading it thus must have been dropped, and the monument upon Mount Ebal must have perished; for in the reign of Josiah, about eight hundred years afterward, the book of the law was found in the temple. How long it had been lost is not expressly told. But, from the astonishment and consternation of Josiah upon hearing the book read, its contents must have been long forgotten so that scarcely a tradition of them remained. We are indeed told, that when the ark of the covenant was deposited in the temple of Solomon, there was nothing in the ark save the two tables which Moses put therein at Horeb. The two tables contained not the whole law, but the Ten Commandments. The book of the law was therefore no longer in the ark at the dedication of Solomon's temple. That is, about five hundred years after the law was given, and three hundred before the book was found by Hezekiah the high-priest, in the eighteenth year of Josiah.

From these circumstances, as well as from the expedients used by Moses and Joshua for preserving the ceremonial law, and the repeated covenant between God and the people, it is observed that the art and practice of writing was extremely rare, and that very few of the people were even taught to read. And, that there were few books in existence, and of those few, only single copies. The art of writing, speaking, and thinking, with their several modifications of grammar, rhetoric, and logic, were never cultivated among the Hebrews, as they were (though not till a thousand years later than Moses) among the Greeks.

Philosophical research and the spirit of analysis appear to have belonged among the ancient nations, exclusively to the Greeks; they studied language as a science, and from the discoveries they made in this pursuit, resulted a system of literary compositions, founded upon logical deductions. The language of the ancient writers was not constructed upon the foundation of abstruse science. It partakes of the nature of all primitive languages, which is almost entirely figurative, and in some degree of the character of primitive writing and hieroglyphics.

We are not told from what materials Moses compiled the book of Genesis (which contains the history of the creation, and of three hundred years succeeding it, and which terminates three generations prior to the birth of Moses himself), whether he gathered it completely from tradition, or whether he collected it from the more ancient written or printed memorials. The account of the creation, of the fall of man, and all the antediluvian part of the history, carries strong internal evidences of having been copied or (if I may express myself) translated from hieroglyphic or symbolical record. The story is of the most perfect simplicity, the discourses of the persons introduced are given as if taken down verbatim, from their mouths, and the narrative is scarcely anything more than the connecting link of the discourses. The genealogies are given with great precision, and this is one of the most remarkable peculiarities of the Old Testament. The rest is all figurative: the rib, the garden, the tree of life, and of the knowledge of good and evil, the apple, the serpent, are all images which seem to indicate a hieroglyphic origin.

All the historical books, of both the Old and New Testaments, retain the peculiar characteristics that I have noticed—the simplicity and brevity of the narrative, the practice of repeating all discourses in the identical words spoken, and the constant use of figurative symbolical and allegorical language. But of the rules of composition, prescribed by the Greek schools, the unities of Aristotle or the congruities of figures taught by the Greek philologists, not a feature is to be seen.

The Psalms are a collection of songs; the Song of Solomon is a pastoral poem; the Proverbs are a collection of moral sentences and maxims, apparently addressed by Solomon to his son, with the addition of others of the same description. The prophetical books are partly historical and partly poetical; they contain the narrative of visions and revelations of the Deity to the prophets, who recorded them.

In the New Testament, the four gospels and the Acts of the Apostles are historical. They contain memoirs of the life of Christ and some of his disciples and the proceedings of some of his principal apostles for some years after his decease. The simplicity of the narrative, is the same as that of the Old Testament. The style in general, indicates an age when reading and writing had become more common and books more multiplied. The Epistles of Paul are the productions of a mind educated in the learning of the age and well versed in the Greek literature. From his history, it appears that he was not only capable of maintaining an argument with the doctors of the Jewish law, but of discussing principles with the Stoic and Epicurean philosophers. His speech at Athens is a specimen of eloquence worthy of an audience in the native country of Demosthenes. The Apocalypse of John resembles—in many respects—some of the prophetical books of the Old Testament. The figurative, symbolical, and allegorical language of these books shows a range of imagination suitable only to be the record of dreams and visions—their language is in many parts inexplicably obscure. It has been—and it is to this day—among the follies and vices of many sects of Christians to attempt explanations of them which are adapted to sectarian purposes and opinions.

The style of none of the books of either the Old or New Testament, affords a general model for imitation to a writer of the present age. The principles and rules for composition derived from Greek and Roman schools and the example of their principal writers have been so generally adopted in modern literature that the Scriptures—differing so essentially from them—could not be imitated without great affectation. For pathos of narrative, for the selections of incidents that go directly to the heart, for the picturesque of character and manner, the selection of circumstances that mark the individuality of persons, for copiousness, grandeur, and sublimity of imagery, for unanswerable cogency and closeness of reasoning, and for irresistible force of persuasion, no book in the world deserves to be so unceasingly studied, and so profoundly meditated upon as the Bible.

I shall conclude here the series of letters which I proposed, about two years ago, to write you for the purpose of exhorting you to search the Scriptures, and of pointing out to your consideration the general points of application. With a view to which, I thought this study might be made profitable to the improvement and usefulness of your future life. There are other and particular points to which I may hereafter occasionally invite your attention. I am sensible how feeble and superficial what I have written has been, and every letter has convinced me more and more of my own incompetency to the adequate performance of the task I had assumed; but my great object was to show you the importance of devoting your own faculties to this pursuit. To read the Bible is of itself a laudable occupation and can scarcely fail of being a useful employment of time; but the habit of reflecting upon what you have read is equally essential as that of reading itself, to give it all the efficacy of which it is susceptible. I, therefore, recommend to you to set apart a small portion of every day to read one or more chapters of the Bible, and always read it with reference to some particular train of observation or reflection. In these letters, I have suggested to you four general ones. Considering the Scriptures as Divine Revelations, as historical records, as a system of morals, and as literary compositions.

There are many other points of view in which they may be subjects of useful investigation. As an expedient for fixing your attention, make it also a practice for some time, to write down your reflections upon what you read from day to day. You may perhaps at first find this irksome and your reflections scanty and unimportant, but they will soon become both easy and copious. Be careful of all not to let your reading make you a pedant or a bigot. Let it never puff you up with pride or a conceited opinion of your own knowledge, nor make you intolerant of the opinions which others draw from the same source, however different from your own. And may the merciful Creator, who gave the Scriptures for our instruction, bless your study of them, and make them to you "fruitful of good works."

Your affectionate Father,
John Quincy Adams

ABOUT THE AUTHOR

John Quincy Adams, son of President John and Abigail Adams, was one of America's most distinguished statesmen who served his country as a treaty negotiator, as both United States Senator and Representative (from Massachusetts), President of the United States, and ambassador to foreign nations. From his youth, John Quincy accompanied his father on diplomatic missions to France and the Netherlands, and by the age of fourteen was a secretary on a diplomatic mission to Russia. Under the influence of his father, European institutions (such as Leiden University), as well as his alma mater, Harvard, John Quincy became proficient in Latin and Greek languages and the Greco-Roman classics. John Quincy Adams was one of the most scholarly and godly presidents to ever served America in this office.

REFERENCE NOTES

[1] John Quincy Adams, *Letters of John Quincy Adams, to His Son, on the Bible and Its Teachings* (Auburn, [MA]: James M. Alden, 1850), 21.

[2] Appreciation is expressed to Internet Archive for the valuable service they have rendered with regard to this text and millions of other similar works. Without their service, similar timeless classics would remain dormant in various forms contained in literary archives around the world. The original bibliographic entry of this work is as follows: John Quincy Adams, *Letters of John Quincy Adams, to His Son, on the Bible and Its Teachings* (Auburn, [MA]: James M. Alden, 1850).

[3] Adams, *Letters of John Quincy Adams to His Son*, 7-8.

[4] The entire prayer may be read at this site: Alexander Pope, "The Universal Prayer," Poetry Foundation, February 6, 2018; https://www.poetryfoundation.org/poems/50590/the-universal-prayer.

[5] This set of books would have to have been published before Mr. Adams' death in 1848. Antoine-Yves Goguet, *De L'origine Des Loix, Des Arts, Et Des Sciences; Et De Leurs Progres Chez Les Anciens Peuples*, 3 vols. (Paris: Sold by C. G. Syffert, in Dean-street, Soho, [1758]).

Made in the USA
Columbia, SC
30 March 2021